How Latter-day Atonement

Copyright © 2025

Gospel Tangents

All Rights Reserved

Except for book reviews, no content may be reproduced without written permission.

(Note this conversation was recorded on Feb. 7, 2024. The interview has been lightly edited for clarity.)

Introduction

Join us for a compelling discussion on Christ's Atonement with Dr. Deidre Green and Dr. Eric Huntsman, co-authors of the new book *Latter-day Perspectives on Atonement*. We'll explore the different models used to understand Christ's sacrifice and take a deep dive into how grace is woven throughout. Don't miss this insightful conversation!

Tags: Gospel Tangents, Rick Bennett, LDS Church, Latter-day Saints, LDS Church, Mormon, Mormon Church, Church of Jesus Christ of Latter-day Saints, Mormon history, Mormon, LDS Church, LDS, Church of Latter Day Saints, Book of Mormon, Deidre Green, Eric Huntsman, atonement, womanist theology, penal substitution, Christus Victor, atonement models, Moral Influence, cross, Gethsemane, Jesus, suffered, succor, elder, atoning, feminist, penal substitution, suffering, suffer, sin, theologian, theology, atonement, grace, works, ordinances, Christ, feminist, repentance, women, good deeds, theology, Jesus,

Contents

Introduction 2
   15 Years Studying Atonement 4
   Models of Atonement 11
   Pros & Cons of Penal Substitution 13
   Objective vs Subjective Atonement 22
   Womanist Atonement 24
   Christus Victor 28
   Is Gethsemane Part of Atonement? 30
   Did Bruce McConkie Get Atonement Wrong? 33
   Womanist View of Atonement 37
   Role of Grace in Atonement 38
   Jesus & Joseph Smith Are Feminists! 45
Additional Resources: 51
   Additional Book of Mormon Doctrines (Val Larsen) 51
   Book of Mormon is Filled with Temple (Dave Butler) 52
   7 Gospels in Book of Mormon (Rosalynde Welch) 53
   Theosis & Temple in Book of Mormon 54
   Isaiah in Book of Mormon (Joe Spencer) 55
   Pentecostal Theologian Reviews Book of Mormon 56
   Don Bradley on Lost 116 Pages 57
Final Thoughts 58

15 Years Studying Atonement

Interview

GT 00:39 All right, everybody. Welcome to *Gospel Tangents*. I am excited to have two amazing scholars of Mormonism. I almost called you Mormon history scholars. Will Bagley[1] got mad at me when I did that. He said he's a scholar of Mormonism. He's not a Mormon history scholar. Anyway, you guys have a great book called <u>Latter Day Saint Perspectives on the Atonement</u>.[2] And so, Deidre, could you go ahead and introduce yourself to our audience and tell us a little bit about yourself?

Deidre 01:10 Sure, I'm happy to. My name is Deirdre Green. I am an assistant professor of Latter-day Saint/Mormon Studies at the Graduate Theological Union in Berkeley, California.

GT 01:22 Awesome. And, Eric, can you go ahead and introduce yourself?

Eric 01:26 Yeah, my name is Eric Huntsman. I'm a professor of ancient scripture at BYU. I actually started my career in classics. So, from 1994 to 2003, I was in the College of Humanities. I did my PhD at U Penn in Ancient History, Greek and Roman history.

GT 01:42 U Penn, you're an Ivy Leager.

Eric 01:43 Yes. But I moved to ancient scripture in 2003, mostly because of a growing interest in New Testament studies. So, I specialize in New Testament Gospels, particularly John. I'm also on hiatus. I'm the academic director of the Jerusalem Center, but because of sad current events, our program is on hold. So, we

---

[1] See https://gospeltangents.com/people/will-bagley
[2] Can be purchased at https://amzn.to/4aGlUAl

came home in November, although my appointment goes through August of 2025. So, hopefully, we'll get to go back.

GT 02:06 Oh, well, yeah, I'd love to tag along on one of your [trips.] Do you do some tours there in Jerusalem?

Eric 02:14 Between the first stint teaching there in 2011 and then having a chance to go back as Academic Director for a few years, the only way I could find to get back, because it didn't work out for my family to go teach again, was to do some of those tours. I had a little bit mixed feeling, about doing the same tours, because I didn't want to be too priestcraft-y, but I love the Holy Land and I love taking people to the sights and teaching there. So, I periodically do tours but won't until after my appointment is finished.

GT 02:43 Okay. All right. So, did you and Thomas Wayment[3] switch places? Because he's in Classics now. Didn't he used to be in Ancient Scriptures?

Eric 02:50 Yeah, so we kind of have mirror careers. He actually was one of the people who touched base with me when I was thinking about doing New Testament Studies and encouraged me to move to Ancient Scripture. And then we were colleagues there for a number of years. And then he has since, as you know, gone to Classics. But we actually overlapped in Ancient Scripture for a good 10-15 years, I think. So, we did reverse patterns. But no, it's not like we just changed jobs. There was a lot of time in between. I had the chance to work with him in Ancient Scripture. He's a great guy.

GT 03:24 Yeah. I love Thomas. He's awesome. I love to have him on. Glad to have you on for the first time. Now, Deidre, Dr. Huntsman mentioned that he got a graduate degree at Penn. Can you give us a little bit about your academic history?

---

[3] See https://gospeltangents.com/people/thomas-wayment

Deidre 03:37 Sure. I did my undergraduate work at BYU. I majored in philosophy but minored in microbiology and planned to become an epidemiologist.

GT 03:48 Oh, me too.

Deidre 03:51 Of course. While serving a mission in South Carolina after graduation, I just had a clear sense that I needed to go to Yale Divinity School. And it was that specific and that's where I did my masters and then ended up doing a Ph.D. at Claremont in Southern California.

GT 04:08 Oh my goodness. Now, I served my mission in South Carolina.

Deidre 04:13 No!

GT 04:14 True story.

Deidre 04:17 We'll have a whole conversation about that later.

GT 04:19 Yeah, I'll bet you that I'm older and that I served before you. (Chuckling) But the whole epidemiology thing, I wasn't a biology major. I was a statistics guy. And I wanted to become an epidemiologist, too.

Deidre 04:35 Oh, so you really were being serious about that. I thought you were [joking.]

Deidre 04:37 No, yeah. My master's degree is in biostatistics. I was I was hoping to become, not Dr. Fauci, but, along those lines. But now I just teach, so, it's good. Well, awesome, very good. So, how did you two get acquainted for this book?

Eric 04:59 Deidre, do you want to go ahead and take that?

Deidre 05:01 Sure. Yeah, it's quite a long story. I was asked to co-edit a volume on LDS Perspectives on Atonement, back when I was a young Ph.D. student about 15 years ago, and was originally paired with another professor, who subsequently left the church and so was no longer interested in continuing on the project. And it was defunct for a few years. And then, fortunately, Brian Birch, who had been the person who first suggested I take on this project, had the idea that Eric and I could work together. And so, he introduced us. I believe I was living in Copenhagen at the time. So, we were just email introduced. We didn't really know each other. We exchanged CV's over email, which is a super nerdy thing to do. But it works for academics. And, so we worked together and we're able to finish it off and bring it together. And I've been really grateful for the relationship that we've built over the years.

Eric 06:04 I don't know why Brian picked me out of the very large pool of people to work with Deidre. I was glad he did. You know, when I moved from Classics to Ancient Scripture, my interest is exegesis, and particularly biblical exegesis. So, I had a particular textual approach to things. But Deirdre is so good at theology, and she's such a careful reader, and she's so well versed in Mormon Studies. Sorry, this is going to be kind of a mutual admiration society here. But she's just got such a good grounding in Mormon Studies, that when she approached me, I thought, "Oh, what do I have to bring to this?" But as many Latter-day Saints, even though I'm more strictly Biblical studies, it's kind of an occupational hazard. You can't not be interested in the Book of Mormon. You can't not be interested in our theology. And so, I was interested in all of these things. And so, I thought, "Well, yeah, I can help vet the scriptural stuff. And she can introduce me to some of the other scholars." This may come out as we talk about it. But our initial plan was to try to do some reprints of some really seminal early treatments by Gene England and others on atonement. And then as our own project got so much bigger, and we had so many great scholars and new stuff to put in, we didn't end up doing that. But it was just, really, a great chance to really approach what's the center. Joseph Smith said, this is what the gospel. It's the good news that Jesus suffered, died and rose again, and everything else in the restored gospel are just appendages to that.

Eric 07:12 And we can talk more about how this project migrated from one possible venue to another. But, as it ended up, because it's an academic press, University of Illinois Press, we were able to do I think things with this, that a lot of times when we're writing in a strictly Latter-day Saint venue, you can't as much. I thought we were able to be a little deeper in terms of our treatment. And I don't want to say freer, because it's not that we're restricted, but just the conceived audience was different. And so, it gave us a chance to really find people and encourage them to approach their particular topic really in depth, and with a lot of openness. Is that a fair way of describing it Deidre?

Deidre 07:35 Yeah, absolutely.

Eric 08:01 Awesome. So, Deidre, this is, like, a 15-year project for you then?

Deidre 08:24 Yes, a labor of love to be sure.

GT 08:30 It always amazes me how long some of you scholars spend on books. Because I'm just like, I can't imagine working on something that long. But I did write something 10 years ago on blacks in the priesthood, and it still hasn't seen the light of day.

Deidre 08:47 Well, I will say, in this case, it definitely was worth the wait. We are both so thrilled with how this came out and the contributors that we had involved and the quality of the work they were able to produce. I just can't get over the fact that we have a J. Kirk Richards painting on the cover. And all these things came together so beautifully. And just as Eric was saying, the fact that it's now in a university press instead of an exclusively Mormon press means that it will get a lot more exposure. And so, this was definitely a case where faith paid off and it was definitely worth the wait.

GT 09:27 Now is this for a Latter-day Saint audience or for a broader audience, would you say?

Eric 09:34 Well, because it's for an Academic Press, we had to really think that through and the introduction, which was in itself quite a project to write. I mean, Deidre and I both contributed essays or chapters of our own to the project, but we had to tie all the contributions together. And so, we conceived of two different audiences. One was for non-Latter-day Saint academics who were interested in Religious Studies specialists who are interested, we call it Latter-day Saint Studies but they call it Mormon Studies. And that's fine in that context. We wanted to introduce them more to Latter-day Saint approaches to atonement. But, of course, we were hopeful that interested Latter-day Saints would read it. So we say we have these two audiences: on the one hand, outsiders who are interested in knowing more about Latter-day Saint positions on atonement, but also interested insiders who want maybe a deeper dive. So, [the second audience was] an educated but non-specialist audience, which in itself was a challenge, not just in writing our own contributions, but in editing the contributions and working with our contributors to make sure--you know, you can't just say so and so, General Relief Society President. You have to explain a lot of things that Latter-day Saints take for granted. But that was helpful, because even dealing with the theology, things we take for granted, you had to reexamine in order to express it in more neutral terms and give the background. And that causes us to rethink what we take for granted, if that makes any sense.

GT 11:03 Yeah, absolutely. Well, very good, because as I was looking at the index--and before we get into the names there. I've got to ask you, Eric Huntsman, what's the relationship with Jon?

Eric 11:16 Virtually none, third cousin once removed. So yeah, as I often joke with people when they ask me that question, I'll say, "Not very close. I still have a mortgage." (Chuckling)

GT 11:30 Oh, that's funny. Because I'm looking at the names here, Ben Spackman,[4] who's a former guest. You did the second chapter, Eric. Ariel Bybee Laughton, I'm not familiar with her. But I do know J.B. Haws. I'll just hit the ones that I know, Jenny Reader, Adam Miller, Fiona Givens, Joe Spencer,[5] and, of course, Deidre Green. That's a pretty good all-star lineup of LDS scholars that I recognize, right off the top of my head. So are there are there other non-LDS scholars who've contributed to this?

Eric 12:07 No, everyone who contributed is a practicing Latter-day Saint. So, they are all people working within the community. Everyone has a specialty, although, Sharon Harris, who did a great chapter on communal atonement in the Book of Mormon is in English. So, they don't necessarily need to be in religion or religious studies, per se. But they all have academic training, and brought something in particular to the project that we thought was valuable.

GT 12:35 Okay. How many of these go back 15 years Deidre? How many of these authors?

Deidre 12:42 Oh my gosh, that would be hard to say. I mean, the book definitely went through a large process of development over the years. So, I don't know, just a couple, really. And that's part of what I mean that I'm really, in retrospect, glad that the project took so long there. There are people who are a part of this book that wouldn't have been 15 years ago, maybe because they hadn't finished their education yet, or whatever it might have been. I just am so pleased. I couldn't be more pleased with the contributions that they each made.

---

[4] See https://gospeltangents.com/people/ben-spackman
[5] See https://gospeltangents.com/people/joseph-spencer

Models of Atonement

Interview

GT 13:21 Very good. So, atonement, I have to tell you. I remember gosh, I'm remember how long it's been, at least 10 or 15 years ago. I think I read a *Wikipedia* article because when we use atonement, especially at church, we all assume that we all understand the same things. And so, I remember I talked to Terryl Givens[6] about three years ago or so, I don't remember. And I said, "Can you talk about different atonement theologies?"[7] I thought he did a great rundown. But for those who didn't see my Terryl Givens interview, Deidre, could you give us a rundown on what are-- to me, there's about five of them. Although, when I read Eric's chapter, I was like, oh, there's a womanist. There's a non-violence one, maybe there's more than [five.]

Deidre 14:14 There's definitely a lot. I mean, my guess, I haven't heard your interview with Terryl. My guess is those are more classical, medieval, Reformation-era approaches to thinking about atonement. My specialty is contemporary theology, specifically feminist and womanist thought. So, the kind of critiques and frameworks that I'm working with, primarily, as a scholar are different, although they're responding to those. I'll say, Delores Williams, who is one of the pioneers of womanist theology, really helpfully articulates, in her work on atonement, that all of these different frameworks that we have for thinking about the atonement, all of these different models grow out of a certain social and political context. That really frames the way that the questions are asked and approached. And so, I think it's really helpful to recognize that those different frameworks just give us a slice or a perspective on an aspect of atonement. They're not definitive in any way, which is part of why we see, in the Book of Mormon, itself, and other parts of

---
[6] See https://gospeltangents.com/people/terryl-givens
[7] See https://gospeltangents.com/2024/03/terryl-givens-defines-atonement-4-of-5/

the LDS canon, you've seen multiple of those models at work together. They're not necessarily mutually exclusive. They get conflated quite a bit, both in our own thinking as Latter-day Saints and within the Scripture. And so part of what Eric and I tried to emphasize in our introduction is, we draw on the Book of Mormon statement that the Atonement is infinite and eternal. Part of what we want to think about in this context is that there are really an infinite number of ways and perspectives to think about the atonement. And all of these frameworks can be helpful. And they're helpful in different contexts and at different times to different people. So, part of what I hope will come from this volume is that people will realize that there's a lot of different frameworks that are possible, that most of the extant frameworks that they may be familiar with have been heavily critiqued and challenged and rethought. But I think that they can all be useful.

Eric 16:27 I think part of the challenge is specialists always will analyze things far more than people who just experienced the atonement. It's not just that theologians now, or scholars of the ages or Abelard and Anselm, the great medieval people who are thinking about this, came up with particular theories.

{End of Part 1}

Pros & Cons of Penal Substitution

Interview

Eric 00:38 What happens is, if it is this infinite, eternal thing that we experience and that we benefit from and yet it is infinite and eternal means the mortal mind can't fully comprehend it. We necessarily fall back on models. And models help us understand what we're experiencing. And because some models make so much initial sense--so, for instance, people say, "Well, mercy can't rob justice and the Book of Mormon talks about how Jesus suffered for our sins." And so that aligns with what we have throughout Christian history called penal substitution. That's the one. And we have some very approachable models that some of our own leaders have given us. For instance, President Packer talked about the debtor theory. Or President Hinckley talked about, "He took a lickin' for me," this idea of substitution. Those work so well, and teaching our children or people in seminary or BYU religion classes, we assume that's all there is to it. And the reality is the Atonement is so rich and so deep that all these different models catch a different piece of it.

Eric 01:41 One of the things we try to establish in the introduction is we think all of these models are important and useful. A couple of our reviews, which, fortunately, have been pretty positive so far, have said, "Yeah, they're showing us all these other ones besides penal substitution." And we have never suggested that penal substitution is not an important, if not vital, way of understanding the Atonement. It's just that there are additional ones, which the Book of Mormon, itself, supports. So, Fiona Givens, she and Terryl talk a lot about the healing aspect of the Atonement. Well, that's built into the Book of Mormon. And there are all kinds of other transformational models. One of our contributors, J.B. Haws, who was focusing on atonement in the Doctrine & Covenants, he took the idea of substitution and by taking the word penal out and giving us another concept that helps us understand why it is so vicarious. He didn't use this term, but the way I've described it to people is J.B., he actually has a model that his wife gave him about jeep-ing and having a problem, their natural consequences of making mistakes. And so I've kind of described that as consequential substitution. It's still substitution. But it's not just that there's some Shylock in the sky out there demanding his ounce of blood, if you've got the *Merchant of Venice* reference there, that it is substitutionary. But one of the things that, as Deidre says, has been attacked through the ages is well, who is demanding the punishment? Is a loving father demanding punishment, or is it a personification of justice, etc.? And so we laid out some of those. Ariel went to town on it, if you read her very deep chapter, which looks at all of these patristic models, Church Fathers approach to it. Even in the late antiquity, in the Middle Ages, there were so many different approaches just trying to catch a flavor of this. I like to describe these different models as being different pieces of a mosaic or different colored pieces of glass in a beautiful window. They're all casting a different light on it. So, we were just hoping we could present people all of these different ways that scripture and theology have tried to explain what Jesus has done for us.

GT 03:44 Yeah, very good. I think, personally, I've always looked at, especially the Book of Mormon and the Bible, and probably Elder Packer, I think, has had the most impact on me and I think [on] a lot of Latter-day Saints with the idea of a penal substitution model, the idea that Jesus paid for all of our sins. I have to be careful, because I'm like, can I say, I don't like that model. It just seems like why would a loving God beat to death a savior for my sins? He didn't deserve it. Because you think of the scapegoat, and that we put all-- ancient Israel, they would put all their sins on the scapegoat, and the scapegoat would take all the sins away from the tribe. To me, that's the only model, in an LDS context, that gets emphasized, I will say. And so, some of these other models, like satisfaction, moral influence, Christus Victor, could we spend a little bit more time on those for people who aren't as familiar on those other different models? Because I've talked to a few people, and they're like, well, the LDS Church doesn't have any official atonement model, which I think is probably true. And maybe, we take a little bit from each of those models. But to me, penal substitution is the only one you see at church. I don't hear Christus Victor. I don't hear any of the other ones.

Deidre 05:28 I would like to make a lot of comments about that. First of all, let me say that, a lot of people share your view that the penal substitution theory just feels really problematic. I want to just name that while I appreciate the reasons for that, if you think about it long enough, even a moral influence theory of atonement, which has become much more popular, and I'll make a point in a moment about how I think actually LDS teachings have shifted in that direction. Even that is quite problematic in its own ways. And so, I want us to think carefully before we actually dismiss certain models. To the point that we were both making earlier, I think all of these models get something right. There is a kernel of truth. There is a point that's important in all of these models. But I don't think it's possible to just choose one or just fault or vilify one of these models. And so, I want us to be careful about that. I think part of what is problematic for people in the penal substitution theory is often just the issue of violence. But violence is a is an issue all the way around when we're thinking about atonement. And you'll see that a lot of the chapters in this volume are not just giving us an alternative to thinking about penal substitution, or hyper focusing on penal substitution, which I think is more of a problem than the model itself. But it's also trying to deal with the issue of violence. When we're dealing with that issue, it isn't to negate that that we believe that Christ hung on the cross or that Christ bled from every pore. It's not to negate that that matters. But for me as a theologian and a scholar, when I'm moving away from a sort of hyper fixation on violence, which I think is sometimes a problem, it's to say that that's not the ultimate meaning of atonement. That's maybe not the most important point. But it's not to negate it or deny it.

Deidre 07:45 I think the same thing is true when you see some of these alternative models that aren't focusing so much on penal substitution. It's not necessarily to deny penal substitution, or that there's anything worthwhile in the penal substitution model. I personally wouldn't be comfortable doing that. But it's to say that, as you're suggesting, Rick, we've hyper fixated on that model, to the exclusion of other facets of atonement, that are problematic. So, I said I would come back to this point about how, I think, really, there has been a significant shift over the last few decades. Eric and I talked about this in the introduction to the volume, that where a penal substitution theory, both in scripture and with the metaphors that Eric was describing earlier, there's been a shift away from that towards more of an emphasis on passages like Alma 7 that give us more of a sense of this moral influence model, and also a sense of Christ's solidarity with our suffering, and Christ's empathy with our suffering. And so I do think that, actually, in General Conference talks, in the church in general, there has been a gradual shift over a few decades, that fits a more popular trend in Christianity, to really move towards the sense of solidarity and empathy that Christ has with us, more than Christ being punished or having to take on this cruel suffering that's imposed on him. Eric, do you want to add to that?

Eric 09:26 I'll jump in. Once again, Deidre and I were quick not to dismiss penal substitution, because I don't think you can, if you're going to take scripture at its face value. But by only privileging substitution of any type, we're missing all these other aspects of what Jesus did for us. Now, atonement, of course, is a neologism. It's an English word. It's not Latin. It's not Greek. It's not Hebrew. But this idea that it's everything Jesus did to make us at one again with the Father. It's not only about sin and death. Now, when I teach Book of Morman at BYU, I talked about sin and death as being the two grand pillars. Redemption from sin and resurrection from death are the two grand pillars of the atonement. They're helping us overcome what Jacob would call, "That awful monster, death and hell." But there are other things that make us not like God. And if I can be personal for a moment, I have a son with autism. Now, that is not a sin. It is a physical situation he's based on. But that's something that will be healed or overcome. I don't believe my god is autistic. Just like I don't think my god is depressed, but I am depressed. I mean, there are a lot of things we experience in mortality, besides just moral sin and physical death, that keep us from being like our heavenly parents or Jesus Christ. Sometimes, and this is where we, as academic geeks, perhaps overly nuance things. But for instance, in biblical translations in the New Testament, there was a big debate over whether a particular word in Greek should be translated as propitiation or expiation. Propitiation seemed to indicate or intimate that we had to propitiate an angry God. And yet expiation means that there is something, the Greek word being miasma, we're experiencing something in mortality, which is diametrically opposite to who God is. And we need to overcome that.

Eric 11:21 Now, one of the reasons why I think Ben's chapter and then mine were helpful to start the project is Ben, for instance, laid out that the most common word for atonement in the Hebrew Bible, the Kippur stem, means the cover up. It's covering these human conditions, this mortality, this moral sin. In the New Testament, khatola gay actually means reconciliation. We're estranged from God for any number of reasons and Christ is bringing us back together. And then when we had the chapters, not just Nick Frederick's and Sharon Harris', but Joe's and Fiona Givens', when she was talking about atonement, the healing aspect, which is such a great Christological, soteriological contribution of the Book of Mormon, if we're only focusing on penal substitution, we're missing the fact that Christ's atonement heals us from any number of things, not just moral deficiencies, not just sin, not even just physical death. Does that make sense? And so, our hope was by introducing the whole spectrum of different models, which are just human ways of trying to understand what Christ has done for us, we meant to open up the richness of what atonement study is, not to replace penal substitution, but add to it. I mean, I think Deidre and I both agree in our work, we're not either/or kinds of people. We're both-and. We just want to be able to plumb the depths and appreciate it more.

GT 12:51 Yeah, and I like that, because I think-- I mean, I agree with you, that all of the different atonement theories have something to offer. And so, I totally embrace the idea. It just seems to me that the LDS Church, especially, I would say, hyper focuses on penal substitution. And so I would love to get away and not talk about that and get into this Christus Victor and some of these other theories. I think, in fact, Deidre, was it you or Eric, one of you said something about consequential substitution?

Eric 13:30 Well, that's how I was trying to describe what J.B. Haws did. So, J.B. laid out from the Doctrine & Covenants, that there are certain consequences: you touch a fire, you're going to be burned. If you go into a mine that's been closed and you fall into a pit, you're going to get hurt. And so, there are consequences to our actions, not just moral volitional things where we make a wrong choice, but sometimes just mistakes we make, and that Christ was absorbing those consequences for us. So, that's the way I tried to describe what J.B. did more eloquently.

GT 14:04 And that's what Terryl Givens said to me on my podcast. He used something, he said, "I need to come up with a new term," but I know consequential was in the term. And I was like, oh, that sounds like Terryl Givens.

Deidre 14:16 Well, J.B. does rely on Terryl's thought quite a bit and springboards off of it to develop his own theory. So, readers will see some threads there, where he's drawing on Terryl's work. And then also going further and focusing on the resources in the Doctrine & Covenants. I just want to--oh, go ahead, Eric. You're about to say [something.]

Eric 14:40 Oh, no, no. I just wanted to follow up one more thing. It's not I'm trying to push back on you, Rick. And it's not that I'm the standard bearer for penal substitution.

GT 14:47 Push back.

Eric 14:49 Two of the people whose works we were originally going to try to reprint in our volume, Gene England's and Lorin Hansen's, we use as kind of models of what could go wrong with taking one approach and why we want to be both-and. Now almost all of us who have read his work, love Gene England, and he was so thoughtful, and he took something which was not unique. He took Abelard's theory, which was the root of moral influence. And because of beautiful passages in the Book of Mormon, he ran with what he called a Latter-day Saint approach to moral influence. But Terryl, in his biography of Gene,[8] pointed out that Gene got some pushback from that from Elder McConkie and others,[9] because Gene focused so single-mindedly, "This is the model," to the extent that he was almost dismissing vital things that the Atonement actually has done for us. But what Lorin Hansen did in his very long *Dialogue* article,[10] I mean, we would have added a lot of pages to our volume, if we had reprinted it, is he pointed out, yes, there are some valuable things to see from moral influence, but we can't step aside from these other ones. So, even if we might personally say, "Well, who's demanding the punishment? Is it personified law? Is it God, Himself? Is it Satan?" If there are some things we can't understand about it, I would say we're, actually, I'm not going to say at our peril, because that makes me sound too doctrinaire. But I think we are risking losing something vital about what Jesus has done for us. I just don't think there's a way [to understand,] not just from biblical scripture, which is my specialty, but from Book of Mormon scripture, about sin and death being the two great obstacles, and mercy and justice. That's why President Packer's debtor model ran with it. Maybe that's why people embraced it.

Eric 16:35 We were just saying, okay, there still some things about that we don't understand. Who's demanding it? How does this pay it? But we just want to understand the richness. The reconciliation model is one that really resonates with me. Now, that's probably because I'm a New Testament geek, and khatola gay means reconciliation. But I remember very early on when my children were

---

[8] "Stretching the Heavens" can be purchased at https://amzn.to/3uo3VM5
[9] See https://gospeltangents.com/2022/07/hard-questions-at-church/
[10] See https://www.dialoguejournal.com/wp-content/uploads/sbi/articles/Dialogue_V27N01_207.pdf

young, my son Samuel had spilled some grape juice on my wife's very light-colored carpet. And we were angry. And the first impulse was, why did you do this? My daughter, Rachel, who's six years old, got in the way and said, "Daddy, don't be mad at Sam." And that gave me enough pause, that I restrained my impulse, and ended up helping him clean it up. We took care of the situation. And later, trying to use that episode in my teaching at BYU, I would say, "If Sam was about to touch a hot stove, and I took him away, and was about to shake him, because I want to teach him a lesson, and Rachel stepped in said, 'Daddy, don't shake or hit Sam, hit me." I mean, that would cause reason to stare. As a loving parent, I don't want to do that. And, yet notice that my natural impulse was to do that. But the idea that someone could step in and bring two parties together, I mean, that's more of a model I resonate with, as a more experienced parent now. Because, as we get older, and our children make different choices than us, or friends or family make different choices, a lot of people step away from the church, for instance, that this idea of estrangement is real. And sometimes it takes a third party to step in.

Eric 18:15 So, that reconciliation model was not one that I heard taught a lot, that meant something to me. And to say, hey, look in some of these Greek New Testament texts, that's really the root of it. And yet, I do believe that some of these things need to be covered, which is what Ben points out when he talks about what atonement means in the Old Testament. And so, I provided two of the only tables we have in the book. And it's because I had too much stuff to write my chapter. But I have these ridiculous tables where I looked up every passage in the New Testament and put them in categories and whatever. But I just wanted to illustrate what I could not explain in the narrative part of my chapter, is that there are dozens of models that Scripture uses. They all have taught me something valuable. This is what we were hoping this book would do. For believers, not necessarily for our non Latter-day Saint scholarly audience, but for our believing insider audience, we wanted them to step away saying, "Wow, Jesus is awesome. Wow, this really is the center of the gospel." When I was trying to explain to my son as he got older with his challenges, he has autism, and I was trying to use the debtor model or the He took a licking for me model, and I was stumped. I said, "Buddy, when we turn this light switch, the light comes on." I can explain in some vague terms, electric current goes and it causes the filament and a light to come on. But what I was trying to point out to him was that I don't know the details and all the mechanics, but I know from experience that when I flip that switch, the light comes on. I just want you to believe, pal, that if you believe in Jesus, and you're sorry for your sins and you ask him to forgive you, it's going to work.

Eric 20:04 And so this is, of course, the tension. The intellectual part of us wants to talk about nuances and details and get all deep and theological. But as practitioners, not just as theologians, the fact is, it works. Most of us, to some degree or another, had at some point in our life experienced that, I don't know if that made any sense, Rick?

GT 20:24 No, it did. And I love that you want to include all the models. I did look at those tables, although there were way too many pages. {group chuckles}

Eric 20:35 The book, when they were doing the book layout, they're like, how are we going to make this work?

{End of Part 2}

Objective vs Subjective Atonement

GT 00:41 But I do like some of the other models. And I like-- because I know, in fact, I just pulled up the Wikipedia article,[11] because I was looking at it. It's really different than the one I remember from 10 years ago when I saw it. But I would like to hit some of the main ones. Could you describe for an audience who may not be familiar with other models? I want to get away from penal substitution, personally. I want to talk about the others, because I think people don't know what they are. So, Eric, you mentioned moral influence. I remember in your chapter, you talked about nonviolent and womanist. And I think Deidre, you're kind of the--you're the womanist [expert.] And is that just another word for feminism, that's not supposed to be as...

Eric 01:28 Deidre, why don't we do this, because you're more of a theologian? Why don't I do the three classic approaches, and then we'll let Deidre do the more theological expansions. And for your listeners who haven't seen the book yet, we divide the book into two sections. The first is called Scriptural Historical Foundations and the second section is called Theological Exploration. So let me do the foundation part and then Deidre can do the expansion.

Eric 01:52 Not everyone agrees with this, and the person who immediately followed me, Ariel Bybee Laughton, pointed out that this is an outdated rubric. But there was a Swedish scholar, Gustaf Alin, who came up with three major theories. And the one was objective, and then one was subjective, and one was what he called Christus Victor. And the objective is an umbrella for atonement models that are trying to change someone else besides ourselves. So, it's either for those who use the term propitiate, propitiate an angry God, or to ransom us from the devil, or somehow change

---

[11] See https://en.wikipedia.org/wiki/Atonement

something else. I mean, J.B. would, even, I think, subscribe to this: change nature and natural law that are demanding a consequence.

Eric 02:40 Subjective models are that the atonement is changing us. And just fast forward to the Givens, healing would be a subjective model, the Atonement is changing us. What Gustav Alin pointed out with Christus Victor, and he had some good New Testament models for this, is that Christ was victorious over something like sin or a death. So, those were the three big rubrics. And we had people in the Middle Ages--Abelard was for--which one was that? He was objective, right? And then Anselm was subjective. This is outside of my ken here. But then we get into many other models. And so Ariel set the stage for that. And then someone like Deidre, who does so much with contemporary theology, was able to bring in these non-violent models. And yes, she'll tell you womanist is very much different from feminist. Go ahead, Deidre.

Womanist Atonement

Deidre 03:38 So, I work primarily as a feminist theologian. So the term womanist refers to women of color, specifically and largely black women. There are lots of different subsets, different names that people will use to specify women of different ethnic and racial backgrounds, with the recognition that feminism isn't a monolith. There's intersectionality, that issues like race, class, different social locations affect women differently. And so, Delores Williams, who I mentioned earlier, was one of these pioneers of womanist theology. She also made an incredibly difficult case against traditional atonement theories, specifically as a black woman, and talked about how this idea of what she called surrogate suffering, where Christ takes on the suffering of other people in some redemptive way, is extremely problematic for women, given the history of slavery. It really fits a sort of model of what women under slavery were asked to do. And so, a lot of my work, starting with my dissertation and going on to the present, is thinking about how our models of atonement are deeply problematic in terms of valorizing violence, or valorizing excessive self-sacrifice or giving us a sense that all suffering is inherently redemptive and good. This makes women vulnerable to abuse and exploitation. It makes them vulnerable to under development, a sense that, almost, they're more righteous if they don't develop themselves as individuals. All of this really grows out of different theories and models of atonement and the way that atonement is talked about. So, I am really concerned, as a scholar, in terms of thinking about what's really efficacious and helpful in the ways we think about atonement.

Deidre 05:59 So just as Eric and I are defending that, all of these different models have some kernel of truth. I also want to recognize that some are more helpful for us to think about. So, coming back to this issue of penal substitution, one thing that I want to name that is really advantageous about a model like that, is that it gives us a sense that the Atonement is absolutely necessary. Now, is it a completely satisfactory explanation about why it's necessary?

Maybe not. There are maybe some issues there that are problematic that we want to play with. But it helps us understand that when Christ is suffering so ultimately, that there's an actual reason that that happens, that there was no other way. Something like moral influence theory, which Gene England, as Eric was saying, made popular within Mormonism over a period of time, maybe not immediately. But my sense is that both within Mormonism and beyond it, there is just intuitively, a greater level of comfort with something like a moral influence theory. But when you really think about it, if we're concerned about the issue of violence, if we're concerned about valorizing suffering in a way that becomes really dangerous and problematic for people, particularly people of marginalized identities, then moral influence theory is actually a bigger problem than penal substitution. I'm going to say this as raw, as I say things as a feminist theologian. If Christ is suffering, so ultimately, just for fun, if this is something that divine beings do for fun, rather than because it's absolutely necessary, that is actually a much deeper ethical problem for us to grapple with. And so, I just really want to name that. I think people are too quick to dismiss penal substitution and too quick to latch on to something like moral influence. There are problems all the way around. And there are really helpful kernels of truth all the way around. And so we really need to be careful in thinking about this.

Deidre 08:14 And so you'll see that in the second section of the book, as Eric was talking about the division, you'll see a lot of contemporary theological approaches to thinking about atonement within the Latter-day Saint canon, within our theology, that move away from a lot of violence and move away from penal substitution. I think that that's the right thing to do. Because I think, as I was saying before, there are lots of ways that we go wrong in our thinking, when we are too fixated on suffering and violence, just as a practical matter. But we also want to have a sense that if this is what Jesus did, if he did suffer in this excruciating way, which I believe he did, we also want an explanation that's better than he just chose to. That actually is deeply problematic, to my mind. I think, actually, we have a more humane view of God, we have a more humane view of atonement, if there is some reason that Christ had to do that. Within the Church of Jesus Christ of Latter-day Saints, within our canon, especially given the Doctrine and Covenants, we have a way to do that. We have we have a concept of eternal law, that there are ways that we just have to do things and even God is subject to those laws. So, we have a way to hold on to this idea of necessity, that Jesus suffered this much because there was no other way, but that it's not some cruel, angry god that's imposing this rule like we get in classical Christianity, that God isn't just having to be placated. But there's something about the nature of the universe, there's something about the nature of existence, that requires this. And so, I just think it's really important that we think really carefully about all these issues and not be too quick to dismiss one view or another.

Eric 10:18 Back to that brief foray I had into expiation versus propitiation. Propitiation became unpopular with more contemporary translators, because propitiation made God angry. But expiation would be in harmony with what Deidre was saying, in terms of Doctrine and Covenants and law. These are just things that happen. In terms of the feminists and particularly the womanist objection to violent atonement models, I think there actually is an application that, Rick, even straight white males can associate with, which is, the problem is when we feel like we have to suffer. Christ suffered, so we have to suffer, right? I mean, this is why the womanist critics were concerned about this. Are we going to valorize all of this stuff that we've had to go through? I can't tell you how many times I, myself, or in the few times I've served in church leadership, I've dealt with people in the repentance process, as we used to call it. "I haven't suffered enough." When the Scriptures say broken heart and contrite spirit, it doesn't mean that we're suffering for our sins. It means our hearts are broken, that we would disappoint God or we've let ourselves down, or we to have contrite spirits, to be humble, to receive the effects of the atonement. We need to come unto Christ. But the reality is, Christ did the suffering. And, yet, sometimes, I think, a simplistic understanding of penal substitution. "Well, Christ had to suffer for those sins. So, I have to suffer this much to receive the grace." Does that make any sense? I mean, I think that's a false assumption we've often had. Because you need to bring fruits meet for repentance, which is the scriptural expression, we feel like we need to suffer X amount before we're forgiven. When really, the broken heart means that I recognize I've done something wrong. I'm sorry, Lord, but I have faith in Jesus, I'm going to come to him, He did the suffering. And see this is why we can't dismiss penal substitution, or in J.B.'s, consequential substitution. There is suffering. But the miracle of the Atonement of Jesus Christ is that we don't need to suffer. And even though we may not understand why there needs to be "suffering," our finite minds don't grasp that, that's the nature of eternal law. And Christ does that for us. That's why we can't let go of substitutionary theories. Let's not just privilege penal substitution. We can't just give up the idea of vicarious substitution.

Christus Victor

GT 12:52 Very good. You know, I talked to Chris Thomas.[12] He's a Pentecostal theologian in Cleveland, Tennessee. And I asked him a little bit about his view of atonement. And it sounds to me, and, hopefully, Chris, I'm not getting this wrong, but you can correct me if I am. It sounded to me like he was much more open to a Christus Victor, where Christ triumphed over death and sin. And I guess that's a little bit related to the ransom theory, that we're paying-- what, are we paying the devil ransom to free us? Then it's like, well, do we want to pay the devil anything? So, I guess there's some problems with that as well. But it is appealing to me that Christ was victorious over death and sin. Let's celebrate that. He's the king. Can you talk a little bit more about Christus Victor?

Eric 13:53 Yeah, and I think, actually, looking at it through a Book of Mormon lens, since we do have those expressions in the early books of the awful monsters, sin and death. And that's kind of described almost as Satan. But I think Satan becomes the representative, if you will, for the fall, if that makes any sense. I mean, Christ is triumphing over the effects of the fall. And I know you want me to address that directly. But there is a subjective model that I am very attracted to, because late Pauline writings, and Johannine stuff, and I'm addicted to John, have a model that is a subjective model, which is participation. Somehow, we're participating with Christ in what he's experienced. And that is changing us. The Givens would say healing. But, Paul would say, occasionally, "I die daily." Well, it's not that the eternal spirit of Paul is dying daily, but rather his sinful nature or his mistakes are dying daily. One of the reasons why I'm so thrilled that we're re-embracing the cross in Latter-day Saint experience in theology, is because what you have is this image of Christ carries not just our sins, but also our heartaches, our sorrows, our disappointments to the cross.

---

[12] See https://gospeltangents.com/people/chris-thomas/

When he died, those things had an end. Does that make sense? And so, it's not just enough to suffer in the garden for it. I mean, they actually have to have an end. And because we participate with Christ, in that moment, our sorrow, our disappointment, our mistakes, have an end. But I think, back to your question, sorry for that little digression there. I just want to get participation.

GT 15:35 We go on tangents here. It's okay.

Eric 15:37 That's what you do, right? *Gospel Tangents*! (Both chuckling) But in terms of how I think we could look at Christus Victor, not as the devil demanding a ransom, but that idea of law. The results of sin and death are fixed. Christ overcame those. So, that would be the victor part of it. He's triumphing over the natural consequences that follow. I would broaden it, not just because of moral volitional mistakes, we choose to do the wrong thing, that 's sin. We might, necessarily, get sick, suffer and die. That's a physical consequence. But I would say physical disabilities or sicknesses or heartaches or disappointments, those things are overcome. Christ triumphs over those. That's where we'd say, by participating, bring that in, those things are healed.

GT 16:36 Deidre do you have anything to add to that?

Deidre 16:40 No, I'll leave it at that.

{End of Part 3}

Is Gethsemane Part of Atonement?

GT 00:47 I want to throw more one more question at you guys, and then we'll dive a little bit more into the book. So, I also spoke with a Lutheran pastor, Willie Grills,[13] and he said, "I have a question for you, Rick." And I was like, I ask the questions. I don't answer questions. But anyway. (Chuckling) So Willie had read Bruce R. McConkie's *Mormon Doctrine*. And he said, "Is it true that Mormons believe," and so I'll throw this at both of you here. You can go back and see what my answer was and see if I got it right or wrong. But anyway, "Is it true that Mormons believe that Christ suffered all of the sins in the garden, rather than on the cross?" How would you respond to that? I won't tell you what I said.[14]

Eric 01:38 I think that there has been a pendulum that has swung. I think a lot of it had to do with in the mid-20th century, Joseph Fielding Smith, really taught a lot about Gethsemane, to compensate for an over stress or focus on the cross. Then, his son-in-law, Bruce R. McConkie ran with that. So, a lot of us who grew up in the 60s and 70s, that's what we grew up with. But if you look at the early teachings in the Church, and earlier leaders, it was, he suffered and died and rose the third day. I mean, that emphasis, I think, was more traditional on the cross. Then with Joseph Fielding Smith and Bruce R. McConkie it swung to more Gethsemane, and I think in the 90s, and in this century, we have something which I think is more useful, we're in the middle. The way I teach this in a New Testament context is the garden is where he took upon himself the burden of not just our sins, but our sorrows, our heartaches, our afflictions, our sicknesses. That did cause suffering, because it was like the crushing of the olives, etc. But he carried that burden to the cross, where they had an end. So, I think what happens is, not only did we, within the church, I think, perhaps focus too much on

---

[13] See https://gospeltangents.com/people/willie-grills
[14] See https://gospeltangents.com/2022/08/rev-grills-on-atonement-theories/

Gethsemane, it also gave a lot of ammunition to people outside the church to say, "You Mormons have got it wrong. You think he just suffered for our sins in the garden," when that's never been what our scriptures--I mean, John Hilton has done a lot of work on this. He's actually done, with some of his research assistants, studies of Latter-day Saint conference discourses, etc. And up until about the 1950s and 60s, you did not have a primary emphasis on Gethsemane. And now starting in the 90s and since, you see something a little bit more balanced, both Gethsemane and the cross.

Eric 03:28 And so I think it's partly a function of when most of us grew up. We grew up and it was a Gethsemane [emphasis.] And, you know, Bob Millet used to also say that it's natural for us to teach to our distinctives. Because we have an understanding of Gethsemane, thanks to Mosiah 3 and Doctrine & Covenants, section 19, that others don't. We really emphasize that. And I would add to what Bob said, I think sometimes we also react--this is not a positive thing. We react against what we perceive as the excesses of others. We thought people were focusing on the cross and suffering too much. So, we were skittish of the cross, and we wanted to emphasize Gethsemane, because we knew more about that. What I like to teach in New Testament context is it's not a discrete one-time atoning event, it's an atoning journey: Gethsemane, to the cross, and then all the way the garden tomb. In the Book of Mormon, atonement sometimes means atonement for sin, but usually it's almost everything Jesus has done. Redemption and Resurrection are both part of atonement. I take that journey all the way to the empty tomb, and maybe even to the ascension, so that you've got a whole spectrum of things that Jesus did. That's why I like to call it an atoning journey. Deidre, take that and run with it.

Deidre 04:37 Yes. Thank you for going first, Eric, because you put that much more diplomatically than I will. I mean, I will just say, I think we have a tendency, within the Church, that we need to guard against, which is to define ourselves oppositionally to other denominations in Christianity. I think that's part of what we see happening there. Eric put that much more nicely than I would have. But I think we have to guard against that. Another example could be a figure like Mary. I mean, we really don't talk about Mary, very often, within the Church. But she's important. And she's important in the uniquely Latter-day Saint canon. I think part of how we account for that is trying to demarcate ourselves from other traditions. And so, I think we need to be careful about that. And just as Eric is saying, [we need to] really embrace all aspects of the Atonement, because they're all critical, and they're all critical within Latter-day Saint theology. And I think it's absolutely right that we hold on to these distinctives, as Eric put it, but also embrace the cross, which is absolutely crucial. I mean, the Book of Mormon talks about the cross extensively. Jacob says, we all need to take up our cross.

Eric 06:06 And participate in some way.

Deidre 06:09 Yes, exactly. So, we need to understand what that means and that it's absolutely central to what it means to be a Latter-day Saint, instead of focusing too much on what demarcates us from other traditions. But I am going to look up your answer now, Rick, and I'm going to use yours next time someone asks me, I'm sure.

Did Bruce McConkie Get Atonement Wrong?

GT 06:35 So, Eric, am I getting this right? Are you telling me that Bruce got it wrong?

Eric 06:42 I would say that Elder McConkie was emphasizing something that was very important and that he felt was necessary to emphasize.

GT 06:51 Okay.

Eric 06:52 How was that for diplomatic?

GT 06:54 That was very diplomatic. How about you Deidre? Did Bruce get it wrong?

Deidre 07:03 I'm not going respond to that one. (All chuckling)

GT 07:04 Come on.

Eric 07:05 Actually, let me jump in here to defend Elder McConkie for a moment. Because even though your friend took out of one of the editions of *Mormon Doctrine*, a particular approach, let's all refer to Elder McConkie's rightly famous final testimony, where he talked about Gethsemane and the cross, actually three gardens. I mean, he talked about the Garden of Eden and then the Garden of Gethsemane and then the Garden Tomb. But remember, he was the one--and he, actually, was the one who first clued me into the fact there's more to the cross than I knew, as someone growing up in the 70s. He said, "On the cross the infinite agonies of Gethsemane recurred. And not that we have favorites, but Elder, now President Holland also gave me more information with that, when he talked. He was the one who actually gave me this idea of atoning journey, when he talked about what Jesus had do single-handedly, not just in Gethsemane, but during the betrayal, during the arrest, how he was alone, even on the cross. He had cried out to His Father. So, I would say, even if they emphasize, for whatever reason, a particular aspect, an older--there was a pattern in the mid-20th century of emphasizing Gethsemane, in the most important speech of his apostolic career, I would argue, that Elder McConkie said the cross was absolutely essential.

GT 08:30 Ok. Well, here, I'll give you the *Reader's Digest* version of what I said. I actually agreed with Elder McConkie. (Chuckling) But Eric, I liked your answer better, that it's more than just Gethsemane, it includes the cross and the ascension and the resurrection, as well. And I like that answer. I think that's great. And I think that we should emphasize that more.

Deidre 08:51 I think one point to make about why both moments are important, too, is we get a sense in our understanding of Gethsemane, that there's something maybe more agentic happening there, that this is something that that Jesus willingly takes on. With the cross, certainly, there's more a sense that Christ is willing, but he's also being subjected, obviously, to the cruel behavior of other human beings. I think there's also something about that, for us to think about, in terms of how we experience suffering, as well. Both moments matter. That part of what Christ takes on in the Atonement, is understanding the experience of being a victim, understanding the experience of being the victim of cruel and senseless violence. That speaks to part of what we experience as human beings and part of what he is able to empathize with. And to use language of the Book of Mormon, to succor us. So, I think, even just on that level, it's really helpful to think about all of these moments being part of Christ's experience, part of what the atonement affects and part of how it supports us and redeems us as human beings.

Eric 10:09 This is a new thought to me. So, I'm not going to articulate it very well, because it's just coming into my mind now. But one of the things the Book of Hebrews talks about is we have this Redeemer who knows how to succor us in our experiences. We have this idea that we have a just judge who will judge us fairly, because Christ has experienced those things. I mean, this is actually where not so much moral influence, but the participation comes into play. Let me just take a couple of other points on that journey. To use President Holland's terminology, it's easy to focus on Gethsemane and it's easy to focus on the cross, now. And we're bringing in resurrection. But what about the in between Gethsemane and the cross, where Jesus could say to us at our moment of judgment, I understand you. I understand where you were. So, Jesus is betrayed by a friend. What woman or man, for that matter, betrayed by a spouse, can say to Jesus, "You don't know what it was like to be betrayed." He's abandoned by his friends. Who of us who's been abandoned can say to Jesus, "You don't know what that's like." He was abused. I don't want to be autobiographical, here, but what fifth grader beat up behind the dumpster by his two best friends will say that Jesus doesn't know what it's like to be beat and spit upon and reviled. Who of us who has been wrongly or falsely judged, can say, when Jesus stood before the Jewish leaders or Pilate and was judged falsely, "You don't know what that's like."

Eric 11:40 See, that's why this model, this atoning journey, it's not just the moment of taking upon himself the crushing weight, our sins, sorrows, afflictions, heartaches, disappointments, which press the blood out of him like an olive press. And it's not just having those things carried to the cross and ending there. But it's all those steps in between, as well. The Doctrine & Covenants says he has descended below all these things. In Alma 7, one of the great Christological contributions to the Book of Mormon, when Alma re-articulates what Isaiah said, and said [that] he knows how to succor. What does succor mean? It's Latin for, not just helps, but runs to help us. Let me bring President Nelson in for a moment. One of the things, because I'm really interested in Holy Week and Easter, for a number of reasons, that's another conversation for another time. But in a project that a friend of mine and I did, Trevan Hatch[15] and I did, we ended with a quote from President Nelson. President Nelson is really big on correct terms and correct names. He encouraged us not just to talk about the atonement as a discrete or abstract concept. He wants us to personalize it, it's the Atonement of Jesus Christ. That's the thing, it's everything Jesus experienced, suffered and did for us, which changes us, which overcomes the consequences, which is triumphing or victorious, et cetera, which is paying the price. I remember, this was actually a nascent thought of mine, long before I heard President Nelson say this. But I remember one semester when I was teaching in Jerusalem, I asked my students--because the atonement just trips off our tongue so easily, mostly because of the Book of Mormon. And we mentioned this in our introduction, that we talk about atonement. I mean, specialists, theoreticians, theologians talk about atonement theory all the time. But most practitioners of Christianity don't talk about atonement as much, because it's primarily an Old Testament, not a New Testament thing. But the Book of Mormon uses that term so much. And so, I asked my students I said, "Next time you're about to testify or talk about the atonement, I want you to not use the word atonement. Find some other way to express what it is." They're like, "Well, what will we say?" I said, "Well, here's a shorthand. It's not very short, the saving, suffering, death and resurrection of Jesus Christ." Connect it to Jesus. Personalize it. Now, this was for an academic audience. So, it's called, *Latter-day Saint Perspectives on Atonement*, but it really should have been subtitled, What Jesus Did for Us, What Jesus Experienced for Us. But I think that's such a valuable, not just piece of counsel, but teaching by President Nelson. It's the Atonement of Jesus Christ, what he has done that make us one with the Father and one with him.

---

[15] See https://gospeltangents.com/people/trevan-hatch

Womanist View of Atonement

GT 14:16 Well, very good. I mean, the thought, while you were talking, there that popped into my head was, well, Jesus suffered all things, and especially with Deidre here, there's certain things as a man that he couldn't have had suffered. He couldn't have suffered childbirth. He couldn't have suffered the loss of a child or whatever. And so, how does, maybe a womanist, or a feminist theology look at those sorts of things? Because clearly, as a man, he couldn't have suffered some of those losses that women experience.

Deidre 14:55 Yeah, I mean, I want to be cautious about that and the claims we make about that and how literally or metaphorically we think about the suffering that he experienced. I mean, the reality is our Scripture intimates that atonement is akin to childbirth. God often expresses God's self, in the Hebrew Bible, specifically, about having this maternal relationship to us and with clear implications around redemption and atonement. So, I want to be cautious about overly limiting what Christ experiences or how similar or dissimilar it is. I mean, I think specifically, as a feminist, part of what we want to think about is, does Christ understand what it is to be marginalized? Does Christ understand what it is to be oppressed? And fairly, yes. I mean, this is a figure who is living in an occupied territory and is murdered in the cruelest manner, in a state-sponsored murder. I mean, there are lots of ways that we can think about the way that Christ takes on human experience that aren't always obvious in the ways that we're thinking about, all the time. And so, I really want to be careful about setting limits on that, that are too literal or overly defined.

GT 16:35 That's good.

{End of Part 4}

Role of Grace in Atonement

GT 00:36 Since I mentioned Willie Grills[16] being a Lutheran pastor, of course, the subject of grace and works has to come up, especially with a Mormon talking to a Lutheran. How does grace and works fit in with the atonement?

Eric 00:58 Do you want me to start with that, Deirdre? (Chuckling) This is a whole other conversation, We're going to have to do a lot of Paul and late Pauline stuff. I think it's actually a false dichotomy, number one. I mean, we're basing ourselves on a sequence of arguments in Galatians, Romans and then Ephesians. And then we're using a proof text in James, when James probably didn't have Paul in front of him. So when James says, "Faith without works is dead," he's not responding to Paul.

GT 01:24 Thomas Wayment[17] told me he was pushing back on that, on the grace, on too much grace.

Eric 01:30 In the context of James chapter two, the works there, are works of charity. He's saying that if someone is naked or hungry, you need to put clothes on him and feed him. So, that's the first thing I would say. But one of the great things we're talking about the changes, in the trajectory of the way we've described the Book of Mormon over the years, when I was growing up, and Rick, you and I might be closer in age than the Deidre is to us. But, we never talked about grace in the 50s, 60s, 70s, 80s, really. We didn't. And we started talking about it when President Benson started making us read the Book of Mormon so much. Right? Because you couldn't get away from what the Book of Mormon was teaching about grace. Back to that earlier idea, we teach to our distinctives, we understood that there's a reason for ordinances and there's a reason for

---

[16] See https://gospeltangents.com/people/willie-grills
[17] See https://gospeltangents.com/people/thomas-wayment

obedience. And so that seems like works to us. And we felt like, at least, some Protestants, particularly evangelical Protestants, born again Protestants are emphasizing grace too much. So we shy away from the grace and we emphasize the works.

Eric 02:30 But when we actually got in the Book of Mormon, if grace is what Jesus does for us, that we can't do for ourselves, it's a gift. That's what it means in Greek, or as Elder Bednar explains it from a Book of Mormon perspective, it's the strength and enabling power of the atonement. I mean, that's the connection with this topic, it's the power of the atonement. The most you can come up with--I mean, I know Elder McConkie had a rubric for it. I mean, he had the pure grace, which is the resurrection. And then he had conditional grace, which made all of us just bristle, which is you have to have faith, repentance and baptism to be forgiven for sin. But the Roman Catholics gave me a model for ordinances, which was helpful, since a lot of times--I mean, we have different kinds of works. Are we talking about ordinances as works or are we talking about good deeds as works. Let's make it ordinances for a while. For the Roman Catholics, their sacraments are conduits of grace. It's the way God has prepared for the grace of Jesus to flow into us. Well, that's exactly what we think ordinances are. You put yourself in a position to receive the grace of Christ. In terms of good works, doing good deeds, I mean, if you don't do them, I guess it's a sin of omission. So, you have to repent of that. But any number of good deeds, taking casseroles to people when there's been a funeral or mowing the lawn or doing your ministering, none of that compensates for sin. So, works as good deeds never take the place of grace. But if we're looking at works as the necessity to conform to ordinances, which God has established for us, that these are vehicles or tools by which the grace of Christ flows into us, that Roman Catholic model of sacramental grace, I think they're not opposed. The ordinance as works, are the way the grace comes to us. I just said a whole lot of nothing, Deidre, fill me out here.

Deidre 04:21 Well, I don't know that I'll be any more concise than that. I have a few different points I want to make. The first, and I think I'm indebted to Joe Spencer, if I'm remembering correctly, and maybe Joe will not want to claim this. But I believe I learned this from him. When we think about 2nd Nephi 25 in the Book of Mormon that tells us it's by grace we are saved after all that we can do. That alludes nicely to what we read in Alma 24 with the anti-Nephi Lehis, where it says it was all they could do to repent. It was all we could do to repent. And so that might be one way of reading what it means in 2nd Nephi 25, to say all we can do is required before grace comes in. But what that means really is repentance. I'll say that, for me, what I understand the works piece to be is really the willingness to receive the gift that Christ makes possible. One way to think about that, how do I show that I am receptive to the gift? Well, I show that through the way I live my life. I show that through the way I exist, and that humility, that repentance, that constantly viewing myself as utterly dependent on God and utterly dependent on Christ. That that's the way that I show that receptivity, because I believe that what it means to be Christian, and what it means to be a Latter-day Saint is something that really is not expressed primarily through words, but through the way that we act and the way that we live.

Deidre 05:55 I will say also, King Benjamin gives us this beautiful sermon, about the atonement. And Eric just alluded to that earlier. But part of what I think we don't always appreciate is that what Benjamin is describing there, when he talks about all these illustrations of the ways that people's lives transform, is that he's been descriptive about a Christ-like life that we begin to live as we receive the atonement. I think sometimes we might be tempted to read that list of changes and transformations as prescriptive, that these are the things we have to do to receive the atonement. Instead, it's a result of how the atonement and grace work on us, that these changes flow out of us. And so, we've had a tendency, for a long time within the Church to focus on the works piece, and have this laundry list of things we have to do before the Atonement is really at work or before we receive grace. I think that's wrong. I think, really, what it is, what the work for us is to be receptive, to receive the gift of the Atonement, to receive the gift of grace. And what that looks like, is recognizing our utter dependence on Christ and having a penitent way of being in the world, and that demonstrates our receptivity. Then as a result of that, as a result of receiving that grace, receiving the atonement, that is really what transforms us and allows us to live a radically different life than we would have without it.

GT 07:32 Very good. I, personally, like Eric said, I think that there's way too many arguments about grace and works and they're just two sides of the same coin. But I had Willie on, so, of course, we've got to talk about it.

Eric 07:49 Well, and Joe via Deirdre has given me something really to think about. I mean, we have to make a long list of what works are. If we have the works of repentance, and then we have sacramental works, and then we have good deeds, which I think most Protestants would say flow out of grace, I mean, we're furnished with good works. I think we throw around works and we don't always even say what we mean by that. Are we talking about the works of faith and repentance? Are we talking about conforming to ordinances, performing them? Are we talking about the good deeds that flow [when we're] trying to be like Jesus? So, I think we're not very thoughtful about what we mean when we have these discussions about works.

GT 08:36 I mean, I know as a missionary in South Carolina, getting called out because well, baptism is a work and we don't really believe baptism is necessary and all your home teaching and all of the laundry lists that Mormons have a lot of things that were supposed to go to. Those were the things that we got attacked [on.] So, ordinances probably not as much as just like, oh, well, you feel bad because you didn't bring the casserole because somebody was sick or whatever. I think Mormons can get really get into a checklist mentality. We do try to cover, we do try to get grace because we're doing all that we can do to get that grace. After all we can do, then I can get the grace. A hardcore Lutheran or born again Christian is like, all you've got to do is confess Jesus, you're good to go.

Eric 09:38 Let me push back on that a little bit, because I don't think Latter-day Saints are alone in the checklist. Theologically, they may say all you need to do is confess Christ, but it's, like, the Protestant work ethic, right? I mean, the people who were the greatest examples of the Protestant work ethic were people who believe in grace and double predestination. But they want to assure themselves that they were elected to grace. So you had to show that Christ had changed you somehow. I think it's a natural human tendency to want to have something verifiable or something that you can recognize. It's like all these things that are as much about boundary maintenance as they are about obedience. We do certain things, we act a certain way, we dress a certain way to show ourselves and others, that we're Jesus' [follower.] And because I did my last few years of high school in Jackson, Tennessee, and I had a lot of friends who were saved by grace, and they were born again Christians. But they were as concerned or more concerned--we were Mormons in those days--as my fellow Mormons were about...

GT 10:40 It's okay to use on my channel.

Eric 10:42 ...not smoking and not drinking, among other things. I mean, so there's still these--and it's not just that you were trying to prove to others that you were saved. I think it's we want to show ourselves. The checklist is useful for ourselves. And yet, this is the beauty of the grace of Jesus Christ. We can come back to this. We're almost out of time here. But that whole, you're saved by grace after all you can do, I think has some good arguments. Dan McLellin has looked at this, theologically, and I think I don't even get to talk on this. You can look at that meaning, after all you can do, it's grace that saves you. But I love what Joe and Deidre have shared with us, after all we can do, which is the works of repentance. As someone who loves the Gospel of John, "If you love me keep my commandments," it's another category of works there. Obedience as a work is because you love Jesus, and He wants you to do this. So I don't know. This is getting a little away from atonement of Jesus Christ, but it is certainly connected to it.

Deidre 11:41 I mean, I'll make one last comment about this. I think part of why we're tempted to lean this way as Latter-day Saints is because we emphasize agency so much. I think overall, that's a really positive thing. We should be thinking about agency and using our agency well. But, I think, maybe a better way of thinking about this is moving away from an idea that we somehow earn grace, which is completely contradictory to the concept of grace, and that [instead,] we avail ourselves of grace. And as I was saying before, repentance and different actions or ordinances, we might think of more as invitations, demonstrating to God, demonstrating to Christ, that we invite them in, that we're willing to receive the gift, rather than thinking about it as a way of earning the gift that is already available, that is already ours.

Eric 12:34 That's lovely, Deidre. I love that idea of receiving. We're receiving the grace, and most importantly, we're receiving them.

GT 12:44 Great. Well, what I'd like to do in these last few minutes is, it looks like you have--here I'm trying to look at the table of contents really quickly--twelve people who have written in this book. We've talked about you and Deirdre and J.B. Haws. Who were the people that we haven't highlighted in this book that we should? What are their contributions? And I love J.B., I need to get him on. I don't know if you guys can help him to say yes.

Deidre 13:17 We can probably help. J.B. was just here in Berkeley giving a fireside based on his chapter for this volume and it was absolutely excellent. So, I think he's all geared up to talk about it.

Eric 13:29 Well, Jenny Reeder, how can we not talk about Jenny?

GT 13:33 There was go.

Deidre 13:33 We have to talk about Jenny.

GT 13:34 And especially, when I mentioned earlier, it's one thing to become absorbed as a thinker or talk about Atonement of Jesus Christ theologically, but then it's talking about experientially, which is what we all want to do. And the reason we invited her--well, there are two reasons we invited her. There is a big lacuna in this work, which is we don't have atonement in General Conference talks. Right? We have different verses of scripture. We have some historical things and we have theological explorations, but there was no way, in this volume, it would have to be several volumes, that we've talked about atonement in Latter-day Saint discourse, official discourse. And so, we knew we couldn't do that. But we wanted to talk about Latter-day Saints describing atonement, not just what Scripture said, or what theologians say. Of course, Deirdre and I are both feminists and we wanted to privilege or highlight some women's voices.

Jesus & Joseph Smith Are Feminists!

GT 14:28 Now, is it okay to say you're a feminist? You work at BYU.

Eric 14:33 Well, Jesus is a feminist, and Joseph Smith is a feminist. I mean, I'm not a political activist. I mean, yeah. There you have it.

GT 14:42 That sounds like a great one liner.

Eric 14:44 But if you know Jenny, you just have to love her work. What she did is she plumbed the archives where she spends her time. And she just gave example after example, of how 19th century Latter-day Saint women experienced and lived atonement. It's just such a beautiful chapter and they did it through worship, they did through song, they did it through struggle, they did it. I mean we don't want to just highlight one contributor. But it's a such a powerful chapter, after Old Testament, New Testament, two on Book of Mormon, Patristic authors and Doctrine & Covenants. But then here is how it actually changed real people's lives and real people whom we don't always talk about or read. So, I love Jenny's chapter.

GT 15:40 Deidre, who else are we not highlighting?

Deidre 15:44 Well, I think we mentioned Ben Spackman. But Ben Spackman is finishing his Ph.D. at Claremont. So, he's working on Mormon Studies there and he also has a background in Hebrew Bible and Near Eastern languages from the University of Chicago. He just does a really excellent job in helping us get a sense of the view of atonement from the Hebrew Bible, especially given his really robust background in languages. Other authors that we have, we mentioned Ariel Bybee Laughton, who is an independent scholar, specializing in early Christian fathers and their thoughts. And [she] gives us a really wonderful overview of thinking about atonement from the Patristics to the Reformation, and how that influences or resonates with the LDS tradition. We have Benjamin Keogh, who's from Scotland, also finishing his Ph.D. very, very soon, actually. He gives us a really a beautiful view of the relational side of atonement and thinking about atonement as absolutely, inherently relational on every level. Benjamin just has so much to offer the Church and is such a profound thinker and so innovative.

Eric 17:12 That's a chapter you have to read three or four times. It's meaty. It's meaty.

Deidre 17:14 Yeah. Absolutely. We mentioned Sharon Harris, who is a professor of English at BYU and talks specifically about the Book of Mormon and gives us a new view of atonement there, that Eric's already described. I imagine your listeners know who Fiona Givens is, and that we don't need to give a description there.

Eric 17:39 Nicholas Frederick did a chapter on Book of Mormon and because we have the Book of Mormon and its first publication in English, we don't have it reformed Egyptian. But he did kind of philological study of the word atonement and atone and how it was used. I alluded to this earlier, I don't think Latter-day Saints realize how frequently we use the term atonement or as President Nelson would say, the atonement of Jesus Christ, but it's because of its use its frequency in the Book of Mormon, to represent everything Jesus has done for us. Nick has some really interesting and important insights. We mentioned before that atonement is not just a Gethsemane and Calvary. It's also the empty tomb. He points out that for many Book of Mormon authors, resurrection really is the biggest part of the Atonement. Adam Miller is actually a reprint of something Adam did. Have you had Adam on your show yet?

GT 18:32 I haven't. Adam must be busy, because I just talked to Rosalynde Welch,[18] because they were co-authors on a book[19] about the Book of Mormon. So he's definitely been busy.

Eric 18:43 So, it was a reprint of something he did before. But it's notes on atonement, grace, and... And it's actually set out 1, 2, 3, 4, 5, 6. But it's just, I mean, the way he thinks, he just moves from idea to idea. I think readers will just find that fascinating. It's not your usual, "I have a thesis statement, and then I'm going to lay out the five sections of my chapter, and then I'm going to have a conclusion." No, you are traveling through the intellectual journey of Adam Miller, which none of us can even aspire to, but he just takes you along from point to point. And that's fun. It's a different kind of chapter. I mean, it's a completely different read.

Deidre 19:19 And he's specifically looking at sealing and eternal families and covenant making as part of the Atonement. So, who else do we need to name? I had someone in mind. Oh, Joe Spencer,[20] who I mentioned in a different context.

GT 19:37 I need to get Joe on, also.

Deidre 19:39 Yeah, he does some political theology in terms of thinking about two different models of atonement that we get from the Book of Mormon and specifically how that relates to our ideas about violence.

Eric 19:56 And Deidre, do you want to characterize or describe your chapter on Enveloping Grace? I mean, it's a great way to end this, the anthology.

Deidre 20:05 Yeah, as you would predict, from what I've said, so far, I'm very concerned about the possible consequences for women

---

[18] See https://gospeltangents.com/people/rosalynde-welch
[19] Can be purchased at https://amzn.to/3TK1bX2
[20] See https://gospeltangents.com/people/joseph-spencer

in terms of overdoing an emphasis on violence for the reasons I named earlier, in the podcast. And especially a lot of my work focuses on this idea of the underdeveloped self. One way to think about it is, as one theologian puts it, the soluble self, the self that dissolves into the projects and needs of others, that is excessively selfless and self-sacrificial. And, of course, as I name in the chapter, this is not a problem that's unique to women. But we tend to think stereotypically about gender. But this might be something that's culturally conditioned in women to a greater extent than men. But to think about how to give us new imagery and drawing specifically, on the LDS canon to reimage the Atonement, as not something that calls on us to sacrifice or to become dissolved or diffused into the plans and projects of others, to not see all suffering and self-sacrifice as inherently good. But as something that actually embraces us and holds us together as individuals and actually allows us the grace to self-develop against the cultural forces that would discourage people from doing that.

Eric 21:33 And her chapter, actually, addresses that earlier issue we were talking about works and grace. I mean, in fact, her title is Enveloping Grace. But I think your concluding section is Enveloping and Encircling Grace and How the Atonement Makes Us Whole, and particularly, not just women, but she uses that as the example.

GT 21:55 Cool, cool. I think this is a great topic as we lead up to Easter, which is just a few weeks away here. And I'm hoping that people will go out and get *Latter-day Perspectives on the Atonement.* I think it's a wonderful book. Are you guys, do you have any works together or separately? What upcoming projects do you have?

Deidre 22:22 Eric, go ahead. You were just naming your current project.

Eric 22:27 Well, I've done a lot on--New Testament Gospels is what I do. But, in terms of family and personal practice, I just love Christmas and Easter. So, I've actually written quite a lot on Advent and on the Infancy Narratives of the Gospels and a lot on the passion narratives and Trevan and I did this rework of an earlier book expansion, an earlier book on the Holy Week. But my big project, which will absorb the next few years, except for when I'm in Jerusalem, is I'm doing a full commentary on the Gospel of John right now. So, that's a big, big project. But I've written quite a lot on John, so I'm trying to pull that together and do an actual line by line. So that's what I'm doing. Deirdre is doing many things. Deidre, you tell us what you're doing.

Deidre 23:06 So, my current project related to Mormon Studies, specifically, is to write on the theology of Eliza R. Snow, for the *Mormon Thought Series*, in University of Illinois press, that Joe Spencer and Matt Bowman are editing. And then, in addition to that, I work largely, as we've said now multiple times, on contemporary feminist thought. I'm currently working on a constructive theology on human flourishing and especially attending to the widespread suffering and injustice and sense of precariousness that we face in the 21st century, and to think about a socially responsible notion of joy and flourishing against that backdrop. So, that's where most of my energy is going these days.

GT 24:01 I feel bad. I go to Mormon History Association and Book of Mormon Studies Association, but I don't think I've seen you guys at either of those conferences. Where do you guys hang out when you're not teaching?

Eric 24:13 Society of Biblical Literature, I mean, because I'm a New Testament geek.

GT 24:18 I need to go to that one, I guess.

Eric 24:22 It's so huge, and it usually holds its meetings in November with the American Academy of Religion. So, that makes it even huger. But almost everyone's there. But you just have to look for them, because it's such a big conference.

GT 24:34 Where's that this year?

Eric 24:36 Oh, gosh, I didn't sign up for this year because I thought I was in Jerusalem.

Deidre 24:40 It'll be in San Diego this Autumn.

GT 24:43 Oh who wants to go there? (tongue in cheek)

Eric 24:44 [Sometimes it's in] Denver, it bounces back and forth.

GT 24:49 Okay.

Deidre 24:49 I'm often on the other side of that at the American Academy of Religion. I am on a steering committee for the Kierkegaard Religion and Culture Group. I specialize in the thought of the 19th century genus philosopher Kierkegaard. And so I'm often at conferences in Copenhagen and other conferences, largely related to his work, as well.

GT 25:09 Copenhagen is harder to get to than San Diego.

Deidre 25:13 Well you should come, that's a good excuse.

GT 25:15 I should come. I'd like to go. I've never been. Alright, well, Eric Huntsman and Deidre Green, I thank you so much for being here on gospel tangents. Everybody, go out and buy your *Latter-day Saint Perspectives on the Atonement*. Thanks again for being here on *Gospel Tangents,* I really appreciate it.

Eric 25:32 Thank you, Rick.

Deidre 25:33 Thanks so much. Take care.

GT 25:36 Thanks.

Additional Resources:

Check out our other interviews on Book of Mormon theology.

Additional Book of Mormon Doctrines (Val Larsen)

Dr Val Larsen says many LDS Doctrines are in the Book of Mormon. Many of us don't recognize them.

876: Theosis in the Book of Mormon
https://gospeltangents.com/2024/07/theosis-in-book-of-mormon-val-larsen-5-5/

875: Abish, Queen, & Heavenly Mother
https://gospeltangents.com/2024/01/abish-queen-heavenly-mother/

874: Ammon, Lamoni, & Theosis in Book of Mormon
https://gospeltangents.com/2024/01/ammon-lamoni-theosis-book-of-mormon/

873: Ammon's Story IS Exaltation Story
https://gospeltangents.com/2024/01/ammons-story-exaltation-story/

872: LDS Doctrines ARE in Book of Mormon
https://gospeltangents.com/2024/01/lds-doctrines-are-in-book-of-mormon/

Book of Mormon is Filled with Temple (Dave Butler)

Dave Butler (aka D John Butler) has written 2 amazing books on temple theology in the Book of Mormon.

887: Does Skeptic See Temple
https://gospeltangents.com/2024/02/does-skeptic-see-temple/

886: Approaching the Veil in Matthew 7
https://gospeltangents.com/2024/02/approaching-the-veil/

885: Lord's Prayer is a Temple Text?
https://gospeltangents.com/2024/02/lords-prayer-temple-text/

884: Don't Make Oaths; What About Temple Oaths?
https://gospeltangents.com/2024/02/what-about-the-temple-oaths/

883: Sermon on the Mount is Temple Ceremony?
https://gospeltangents.com/2024/02/sermon-on-the-mount-temple/

882: See Jesus Like Denver Snuffer?
https://gospeltangents.com/2024/02/see-jesus-like-denver-snuffer/

881: Meet Dave Butler
https://gospeltangents.com/2024/02/meet-dave-butler/

7 Gospels in Book of Mormon (Rosalynde Welch)

Rosalynde Welch & Adam Miller are co-authors of the "Seven Gospels of the Book of Mormon."

861: What's in Gospel of Brother of Jared
https://gospeltangents.com/2023/12/gospel-brother-of-jared/

860: Gospels of Abinadi & Samuel the Lamanite
https://gospeltangents.com/2023/12/gospels-abinadi-samuel-the-lamanite/

859: Atonement Theology in Gospels of Mary, Mosiah, Abinadi
https://gospeltangents.com/2023/12/atonement-theology-gospels-mary-mosiah/

858: 7 Gospels of Book of Mormon
https://gospeltangents.com/2023/12/7-gospels-book-of-mormon/

Theosis & Temple in Book of Mormon

Val Larsen discusses theosis & heavenly mother in the Book of Mormon.

779: Satan is Fruit of Tree Knowledge?
https://gospeltangents.com/2023/06/satan-fruit-of-tree-of-knowledge/

2:23:10 Christ Baptized for World
2:37:34 Moral Exemplar Atonement
2:46:19 Satan is Fruit of Tree Knowledge?
2:51:15 Divine Mother in Temple
3:13:00 Pushing Back
3:37:18 Will Val Get in Trouble?

778: Temple is Great & Spacious Building?
https://gospeltangents.com/2023/06/temple-is-great-spacious-building/

1:15:03 Book of Mormon Theosis
1:36:50 Asherah – Divine Mother
1:45:52 Temple is Great & Spacious Building?
1:56:34 Why Laman & Lemuel tried to Kill Nephi (Mother in Heaven)
2:06:03 Nephi's Dream

777: Lehi Was Polytheist? (Val Larsen)
https://gospeltangents.com/2023/06/was-lehi-a-polytheist/

0:00 Intro to Val Larsen
8:00 God is the Author of Evil?
14:55 What Orthodox Christians Get Wrong about God
28:42 Theosis & Heavenly Mother in Book of Mormon
37:21 Israelite Polytheism
50:39 Divine Mother
55:43 First Biblical Forgery?

Isaiah in Book of Mormon (Joe Spencer)

Dr Joseph Spencer is Pres of Book of Mormon Studies Assoc & teaches philosophy at BYU.

927: Time to Dump KJV?
https://gospeltangents.com/2024/05/time-to-dump-kjv-3-3/

926: Contradictions in Nephi & Abinadi
https://gospeltangents.com/2024/05/contradictions-nephi-abinadi-2-3/

925: Is Abinadi Trinitarian?
https://gospeltangents.com/2024/04/is-abinadi-trinitarian-1-of-3/

Pentecostal Theologian Reviews Book of Mormon

Dr. Christopher Thomas teaches at the Pentecostal Theological Seminary in Cleveland, TN and has written "A Pentecostal Reads the Book of Mormon."

585: Comparing Mormons & Pentecostals
https://gospeltangents.com/2021/11/comparing-mormons-pentecostals/

584: Pentecostals in Book of Mormon
https://gospeltangents.com/2021/11/pentecostals-book-of-mormon/

583: Troubling Stories in Scripture
https://gospeltangents.com/2021/11/troubling-stories-in-scripture/

582: Protestant Theology in Book of Mormon?
https://gospeltangents.com/2021/11/protestant-theology-book-of-mormon/

581: Tongue-Speech in Book of Mormon
https://gospeltangents.com/2021/11/tongue-speech-book-of-mormon/

580: Pentecostal View of Book of Mormon Theology
https://gospeltangents.com/2021/11/pentecostal-book-mormon-theology/

579: Is Book of Mormon a Pacifist Book?
https://gospeltangents.com/2021/11/is-book-of-mormon-pacifist-text/

578: Pentecostal Theologian Gives Book of Mormon the Bible Treatment
https://gospeltangents.com/2021/11/pentecostal-bom-bible-treatment/

Don Bradley on Lost 116 Pages

Don Bradley is Author of "Lost 116 Pages" where he details what is missing from the Book of Mormon.

365: Apologists & Critics
https://gospeltangents.com/2020/01/critics-apologists/

364: New Insights on Liahona
https://gospeltangents.com/2020/01/more-details-liahona/

363: How Did Nephi Get Priesthood?
https://gospeltangents.com/2020/01/how-nephites-get-priesthood/

362: Who Stole the Manuscript?
https://gospeltangents.com/2020/01/who-stole-lost-116-pages/

361: Exonerating Lucy Harris
https://gospeltangents.com/2020/01/exonerating-lucy-harris/

360: Masonic Golden Plates & Temple Theology
https://gospeltangents.com/2020/01/masonic-golden-plates-temple/

359: Temple Endowment in Lost Pages
https://gospeltangents.com/2020/01/temple-endowment-in-lost-pages/

358: Laban Killed During Passover
https://gospeltangents.com/2020/01/laban-killed-during-passover/

357: More than 116 Pages Lost?
https://gospeltangents.com/2020/01/more-than-116-pages-lost/

356: How Much of BoM is Missing?
https://gospeltangents.com/2020/01/what-missing-lost-pages/

Final Thoughts

You can get our transcripts at our amazon.com author page. I've got a link here, but just do a search for Gospel Tangents interview, and you should be able to find a bunch of them there. Please subscribe at Patreon.com/gospeltangents. For $5 a month, you can hear the entire interview uncut and for $10 you can get a pdf copy. We've also got a $15 tier where if you want a physical copy, I'll be the first to send it to you, so please subscribe at Patreon or on our website at Gospeltangents.com. For our latest updates, please like our page at facebook.com/Gospeltangents and also check our twitter updates Gospel tangents. Please subscribe on our apple podcast page tinyurl.com/GospelTangents, or you can subscribe on your android device. Just do a search for Gospel Tangents. Thanks again for listening. Click here to subscribe, here for transcript and over here we've got some more of our great videos. Thanks again.

Made in the USA
Columbia, SC
07 June 2025